The Journeys of
Sojourner
Truth

by Barbara R. Moore

HOUGHTON MIFFLIN   BOSTON

Contents

Introduction

Nine-year-old Belle was frightened and confused. She and her little brother stood in the master's front yard. Nearby, some men were talking. The children, who spoke only Dutch, could not understand the words being spoken. Belle's mother and father were crying. They were being held back at the gate.

Belle knew only that the master had died. For months, she had heard talk of a sale. Today, his property was being sold. As an enslaved child, Belle was a white man's property. She was sold to the highest bidder. That day she was taken away from everyone and everything she knew.

Chapter 1

 # Cruelty and Faith

Belle's full name was Isabella. Enslaved African Americans didn't have last names of their own. If a last name was needed, they used the last name of their master. Belle used the last name of Baumfree (BAWM free).

Belle was born in 1797 in New York State. She had five different masters by the time she was 30. By then, she had grown to be six feet tall. She stood straight and strong. Her voice was deep and commanding.

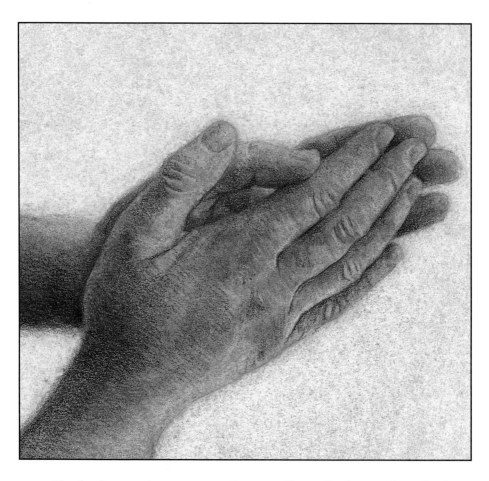

She had great inner strength, too. She relied on a deep faith in God. She remembered her mother's stories. Her mother had told her that God would hear her and help her. When she was suffering and lonely, she prayed and thought deeply.

Not all of her prayers seemed to be answered, though. All too often, her owners were cruel. She was beaten even though she worked hard. Still, Belle kept talking to God.

4

Freedom at Last

In 1817 the state of New York voted to free enslaved African Americans. However, they did not actually receive their freedom until July 4, 1827. But before that happy day arrived, Belle's owner did something she could never forgive. He sold her youngest son, Peter.

Belle was so upset that she ran away. She lived with a Quaker family until she became free. Quakers are members of a religious society who believe in leading simple lives. She learned Peter had been sold illegally to a man in Alabama. In the South, Peter would not be freed. The Quaker family helped her win a lawsuit (a case brought before a court for settlement). She got her son back!

At age 30, Belle had journeyed from slavery to freedom. A greater journey was about to begin.

Chapter 2

 ## A Truthful Traveler

    Until 1843 Belle lived in New York and worked as a paid servant. One day, she believed she heard God speak to her. God told her to become a traveling preacher and to take the name *Sojourner* (SOH jur nur), which means "traveler." She would "travel up and down the land showing the people their sins and being a sign unto them."

For her last name, Belle chose *Truth*. For the rest of her life, she was to tell everyone the truth. Sojourner Truth wrapped her hair in a white turban. She wore a simple gray dress. Dressed in this way and standing so tall, Sojourner made a strong impression on people. At age 46, she set out walking.

Enslaved African Americans fleeing the South

A Strong Speaker

Sojourner slept in sheds or under the stars. She gave speeches everywhere she could. Often, she drew large crowds. Her voice seemed to cast a spell on listeners. She knew long passages of the Bible by heart. She sang hymns and songs she made up. She knew about the suffering of enslaved African Americans, so her words had a great effect. She said that, as Christians, her listeners should oppose slavery.

Chapter 3

 # Life in Northampton

Sojourner found her way to a community in
Northampton, Massachusetts. It was special. Here, people
of all religions, races, and backgrounds lived and worked.
Here, she met a former enslaved African American, Frederick
Douglass. He was beginning to speak out for abolition
(a buh LISH uhn), which was a movement to end slavery.
She also met another well-known abolitionist, William
Garrison. Sojourner decided she would also speak out to
end slavery.

William Garrison   **Frederick Douglass**

Telling Her Story

She told the story of her life to Olive Gilbert. Gilbert wrote Sojourner's story for her. Sojourner could neither read nor write.

The Narrative of Sojourner Truth: A Northern Slave sold well. First published in 1850, it was the first book to tell about life as a slave from the words of an enslaved African American. Sojourner used the money to buy a house and to pay for her travel costs.

A fugitive is someone who is hunted for escaping. In 1851 the nation passed the Fugitive (FYOO jih tihv) Slave Law. This law required people to return runaway slaves to their owners. Many northerners were outraged. More and more people were in favor of abolition.

$100 REWARD!

RANAWAY

From the undersigned, living on Current River, about twelve miles above Doniphan, in Ripley County, Mo., on 2nd of March, 1860, A NE GRO MAN, about 30 years old, weighs about 160 pounds; high forehead, with a scar on it; had on brown pants and coat very much worn, and an old black wool hat; shoes size No. 11.

The above reward will be given to any person who may apprehend this said negro out of the State; and fifty dollars if apprehended in this State outside of Ripley county, or $25 if taken in Ripley county.

APOS TUCKER.

Speaking Out

Sojourner was busier than ever. She gave many lectures, or speeches. Some were to convince people that slavery must be stopped. Others were to convince people that women should have the right to vote.

Many men and women opposed such speakers. Sometimes violent mobs gathered. They heckled, or yelled insults at, the speakers. They threw stones. Some even threatened the speakers with knives and guns.

At one lecture, a man in the audience spoke hatefully. He said that women were weak. They even had to be helped into carriages, he said. Sojourner Truth rose to her full height and began to speak:

Nobody ever helps me into carriages, or over mud puddles, or gives me any best place! And ain't I a woman? Look at me! Look at my arm! I have plowed, and planted, and gathered into barns, and no man could head [do better than] me! And ain't I a woman? I could work as much and eat as much as a man (when I could get it), and bear the lash [whip] as well! And ain't I a woman? I have borne thirteen children, and seen them most all sold off to slavery, and when I cried out with my mother's grief, none but Jesus heard me! And ain't I a woman?

Even the strongest critics in the audience were silent. Hundreds of supporters rushed forward to shake her hand and congratulate her.

Statue of Sojourner Truth in Northampton, Massachusetts

Chapter 4

 # An End to Slavery

Argument and conflict over slavery continued. The nation moved toward war. By then, Sojourner was living in Michigan, where two of her daughters had settled.

When the Civil War began, Sojourner raised money for African American Union soldiers. On January 1, 1863, the Emancipation Proclamation became law. This law ended slavery once and for all.

African American Union soldiers

Sojourner went to Washington, D.C., so that she could help newly freed enslaved African Americans who had come north. They were not yet used to freedom and were still treated poorly. They lived in tents and shacks.

In 1864 Sojourner received a special invitation to meet with President Abraham Lincoln. Lincoln was thankful for what she had done to fight slavery and to help the Union army. She thanked him for helping to free enslaved African Americans.

A Continuing Journey

Sojourner's journey was not yet finished. She worked to end segregation, or separation of the races. She argued that land in the West should be given to freed African Americans. That way, they would be able to make a living. Her requests were ignored.

Sojourner Truth continued to speak out. She spoke in favor of voting rights for women and African Americans.

In November 1883, she died. For 40 years she had done difficult, dangerous work. But she believed it was "the Lord's work." She had won the respect and admiration of a nation.